A Kid's Guide to
Israel

Curious Kids Press • Palm Springs, CA
www.curiouskidspress.com

A WORD TO PARENTS

CURIOUS KIDS PRESS is passionate about helping young readers expand and enhance their understanding about countries and cultures around the world. While actual real-world experiences with other countries and cultures may have the most profound positive effect on children and pre-teens, we understand such experiences are not always possible. That's why our two series of books — "A Kid's Guide to . . ." (for ages 9-12) and "Let's Visit . . ." (for ages 6-8) — are designed to bridge that gap and help young readers explore the wonderful world of diversity in everything from food and holidays to geography and traditions. We hope your young explorers enjoy this adventure into the awesome country of Israel.

COVER PHOTO: Israel camel on a hill with Dead Sea in the background.

Publisher: Curious Kids Press, Palm Springs, CA 92264.
Designed by: Michael Owens
Editor: Sterling Moss
Copy Editor: Janice Ross

Copyright © 2023 by Curious Kids Press. All rights reserved. Except that any text portion of this book may be reproduced – mechanically, electronically, by hand or any other means you can think of – by any kid, anywhere, any time. For more information: info@curiouskidspress.com

Table of Contents

Chapter 1
- Welcome to Israel 4
- Your Passport to Israel 5
- Where in the World Is Israel 6
- Where in the World Is the Middle East 7
- A Brief History of Israel 8
- Cool Facts About Israel 10

Chapter 2
- People, Customs, and Traditions 12

Chapter 3
- Landmarks and Attractions 24

Chapter 4
- The Wildlife of Israel 34

- The IUCN Red List 42
- For Parents and Teachers 46

Chapter 1

"SHALOM" Welcome to Israel

Israel is one of the smallest countries in all of Asia. Yet, it is home to more Jewish people than anywhere else in the world.

The young country is both fascinating and complicated. It is, for example, the birthplace of several Western religions, all of which call the Israeli city of Jerusalem their holiest site.

Sadly, the history of this young country is filled with conflict and wars. Yet, despite the conflict, everyday life in Israel is similar to the United States, Canada, or Western Europe.

You can read more about this fascinating country in this book. Shalom!

Your Passport to Israel

Official Name: State of Israel.
Capital: Jerusalem.
Country Area (Size): 8,550 square miles (22,145 square kilometers).
Population: About 9 million (about the same as New Jersey).
Government Type: Parliamentary democracy.
Official Languages: Hebrew, Arabic.
Money: Shekel.

Photo: Zachi Evenor

The national flag of Israel features a blue hexagram (six-pointed geometric star figure) on a white background.

The hexagram is known as the Star of David. It's a symbol of the Jewish people and of Judaism. It is centered between two horizontal blue stripes or bands near the top and bottom edges of the flag.

The blue color varies from flag to flag, ranging from navy blue to very light blue. The basic design is similar to a traditional Jewish prayer shawl, called a *tallit*.

Where in the World Is Israel?

Israel is a small country in the Middle East. It borders four different countries. To the east are Jordan and Syria. Lebanon serves as the northern border and Egypt borders in the south. Palestine is also to the east.

Many people agree that Palestine is made up of two regions: the Gaza Strip and the West Bank. The Gaza Strip borders Egypt, Israel, and the Mediterranean Sea.

The West Bank is located between Israel and Jordan. It covers an area of approximately 2,270 square miles (5,900 square kilometers). That's about the size of Delaware. Most of the people who live in the territory are Palestinian Arabs.

Many countries recognize Palestine as a sovereign state, but many others, including the U.S., do not.

The map shows the State of Israel and two distinct regions that make up Palestine, as well as the countries and bodies of water that are nearby and/or surrounding.

Where in the World Is The Middle East?

The Middle East is the region around the southern and eastern shores of the Mediterranean Sea. It includes the countries that are located where the continents of Europe, Asia, and Africa meet. Some of those countries include Turkey, Egypt, Iran, Iraq, and Saudi Arabia, among others.

This map of the Middle East shows how small the country of Israel is in relation to the countries around it.

A Very Brief History of Israel

The story of modern Israel begins more than 3,500 years ago. Read how these curious kids tell about the history of Israel.

In the 1700s BCE, a group of tribes, known as Israelites, moved from their home in Mesopotamia (now the country of Iraq) to a land called Canaan, where the Philistines lived.

Hundreds of years later, in about 1000 BCE, the Israelites conquered the Philistines for control of Canaan, roughly the area of modern-day Israel.

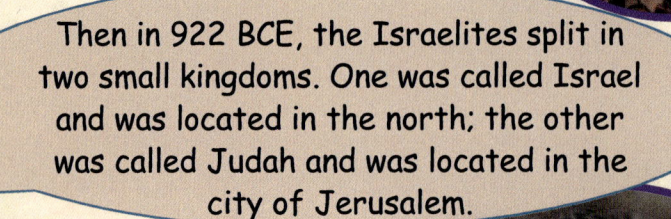

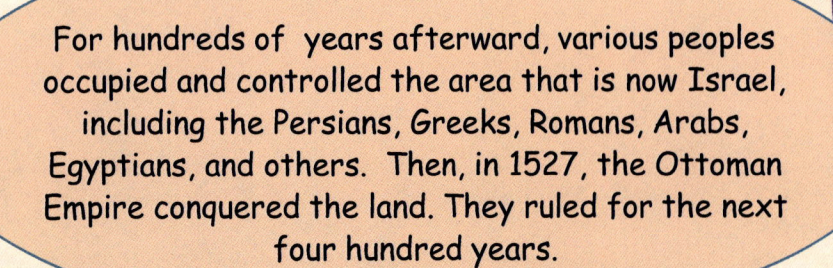

Then in 922 BCE, the Israelites split in two small kingdoms. One was called Israel and was located in the north; the other was called Judah and was located in the city of Jerusalem.

For hundreds of years afterward, various peoples occupied and controlled the area that is now Israel, including the Persians, Greeks, Romans, Arabs, Egyptians, and others. Then, in 1527, the Ottoman Empire conquered the land. They ruled for the next four hundred years.

In 1917, Britain conquered the area from the Ottomans during World War I. Britain supported a "national home for the Jewish people."

From 1939 to 1945, during World War II, the Nazi party in Germany murdered about six million Jewish men, women, and children. Some Jews escaped to modern-day Israel and other countries.

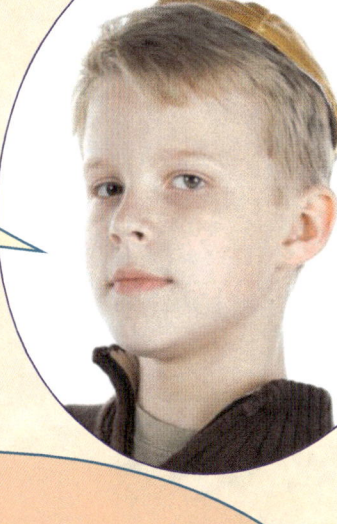

Long before World War II, in 1897, a group of Jewish people launched a movement to create their own state in present-day Israel. Finally, in 1948, the State of Israel declared its independence from Britain.

In the many decades since Israel declared its independence, there have been many wars and acts of violence between Arabs and Jews. Today, the tensions and hostilities continue. Yet, people around the world hope for a lasting peace in the future.

Cool Facts About Israel

The Negev Desert in southern Israel receives only 1 inch (32 mm) of rain a year. By comparison, a town in northeast India gets, on average, 467 inches (11,871 millimeters) of rain each year.

The Dead Sea is bordered by Jordan to the east and the West Bank and Israel to the west. It is the lowest point on the earth's surface. It is 1,365 (416 meters) below sea level.

The 5 Largest Cities in Israel

City	Population
Jerusalem*	882,652
Tel Aviv	438,818
Haifa	279,591
Rishon LeZion	246,323
Petah Tikva:	236,169

*Jerusalem is claimed by both Israel and Palestine. Neither claim is recognized completely by the international community.

McDonald's restaurant in the middle of the desert, near the Dead Sea, Israel

What Does SHALOM Mean?

Merriam-Webster says, simply, that Shalom is "used as a Jewish greeting and farewell." But one songwriter believes it means much more. He wrote:

"It means a million lovely things,
Like peace be yours,
Welcome home.
And even when you say goodbye,
You say goodbye with Shalom."
From the Broadway musical "Milk and Honey" with music and lyrics by Jerry Herman.

As much as 60 percent of Israel's landmass is desert.

The cherry tomato was invented in Israel.

Did You Know?

In summer, the Mediterranean Sea has an average temperature of about 86 degrees F (30 degrees C). It's like getting into a warm bathtub.

2 MILLION The number of trees that have been planted in Israel in the last 60 years.

Nearly 27 percent of the population of Israel is under the age of 14.

Chapter 2

People, Customs, and Traditions

What do you love about Israel?

Jerusalem

A city considered holy by three of the world's largest religions.

Jerusalem is the capital of Israel. It is one of the oldest cities in the world. It is also considered by many to be one of the holiest places in the world.

Three of the world's largest religions consider Jerusalem holy. Jews believe the Messiah will one day appear here; Muslims believe that Muhammad ascended to heaven from here; and Christians believe this is where Jesus Christ rose from the dead.

This holy city is also the site of cherished shrines for these three world religions. Here are three of those shrines.

The Church of the Holy Sepulchre

The Church of the Holy Sepulchre is a holy place in Jerusalem for Christians. That's because the church was built on the place where Christians believe Jesus was killed, buried, and then resurrected, or raised from the dead.

The Church of the Holy Sepulcher is the most sacred site in the world for millions of Christians.

The Dome of the Rock

The dome of the Rock is located on Temple Mount, a hill in the Old City of Jerusalem that is considered a holy site in Judaism, Christianity, and Islam.

The Dome of the Rock is a monument in Jerusalem that Muslims consider holy. It's the oldest surviving Islamic building. Muslims believe it marks the place where an angel carried Muhammad, the founder of Islam, up to heaven.

The Western Wall

The Western Wall in Jerusalem is considered a holy place of prayer for Jews. The wall was part of the Second Temple of Jerusalem, which was destroyed by the Romans in 70 CE. The Western Wall is all that remains.

The Western Wall is sometimes called the Wailing Wall because many Jews pray and weep at the site of the destroyed Temple.

The Sea of Galilee

The place to see historical sites, Biblical sites, and gorgeous nature.

People come to Israel for many reasons. Some may want to see the ancient historical sites; others want to see the New Testament Biblical sites; others come to simply enjoy Israel's beautiful nature.

There's one place they can do all that. That place is the Sea of Galilee, a freshwater "lake" (not a sea). It is the lowest freshwater lake on Earth and the second-lowest lake in the world (after the Dead Sea, a saltwater lake, too, not a sea).

There are many historical and spiritual sites around the lake. For example, it is the place where Jesus performed miracles according to the New Testament, such as his walking on water, calming the storm and feeding the multitude.

The Maccabiah Games
An "Olympics" event for Jews around the world.

You probably know all about the Olympics—the international sporting events featuring summer and winter sports competitions. Thousands of athletes from around the world participate in a variety of competitions.

But there's another version of the Olympics that you may not know about. It's called the Maccabiah Games. It's held in Israel every four years.

Since 1932, the Maccabiah Games has brought together thousands of Jewish athletes from all over the world. The event is also open to all Israeli citizens regardless of their religion.

In 2022, more than 10,000 Athletes from eighty different countries competed in forty-seven sports, including soccer, basketball, table tennis, and (surprise!) chess.

Just like at the Olympics, the Maccabiah starts out with an elaborate opening ceremony. Athletes march into the stadium, country by country, in a "Parade of Nations."

Many Jewish athletes at the Maccabiah Games went on to win big at the Olympics. One was American swimmer Mark Spitz. The 1965 Maccabiah Games was Mark's first international competition.

Seven years later, at the 1972 Olympics in Munich, Germany, Spitz won seven gold medals. Some say he is the greatest swimmer in history. And for Spitz, it all started at the Maccabiah Games.

The Bedouins

A nomadic tribe that has lived in Israel's Negev desert for hundreds of years.

The Bedouins are a group of nomadic tribes. They have lived in Middle Eastern deserts for centuries — long before modern countries were formed. Many tribes still dwell in areas that are today known as Saudi Arabia, Jordan, Oman, Egypt and Israel.

The Bedouins of Israel live in the Negev Desert. They typically follow a semi-nomadic lifestyle. As animal herders, they migrate into the desert during the rainy season and return to cultivated land in the dry summer months.

The Bedouin organize themselves around clans. Each family in the clan is headed by the father, known as a *sheikh*. It's not unusual for a Bedouin man to father several dozen children with different wives.

Today, around half the Bedouin people of the Negev live in seven different towns in the northern Negev. The remaining 50 percent prefer to continue to live a traditional lifestyle. Their living conditions, however, are difficult. Many live without electric, sewage, or water systems.

Holidays in Israel
From Passover to Hanukkah.

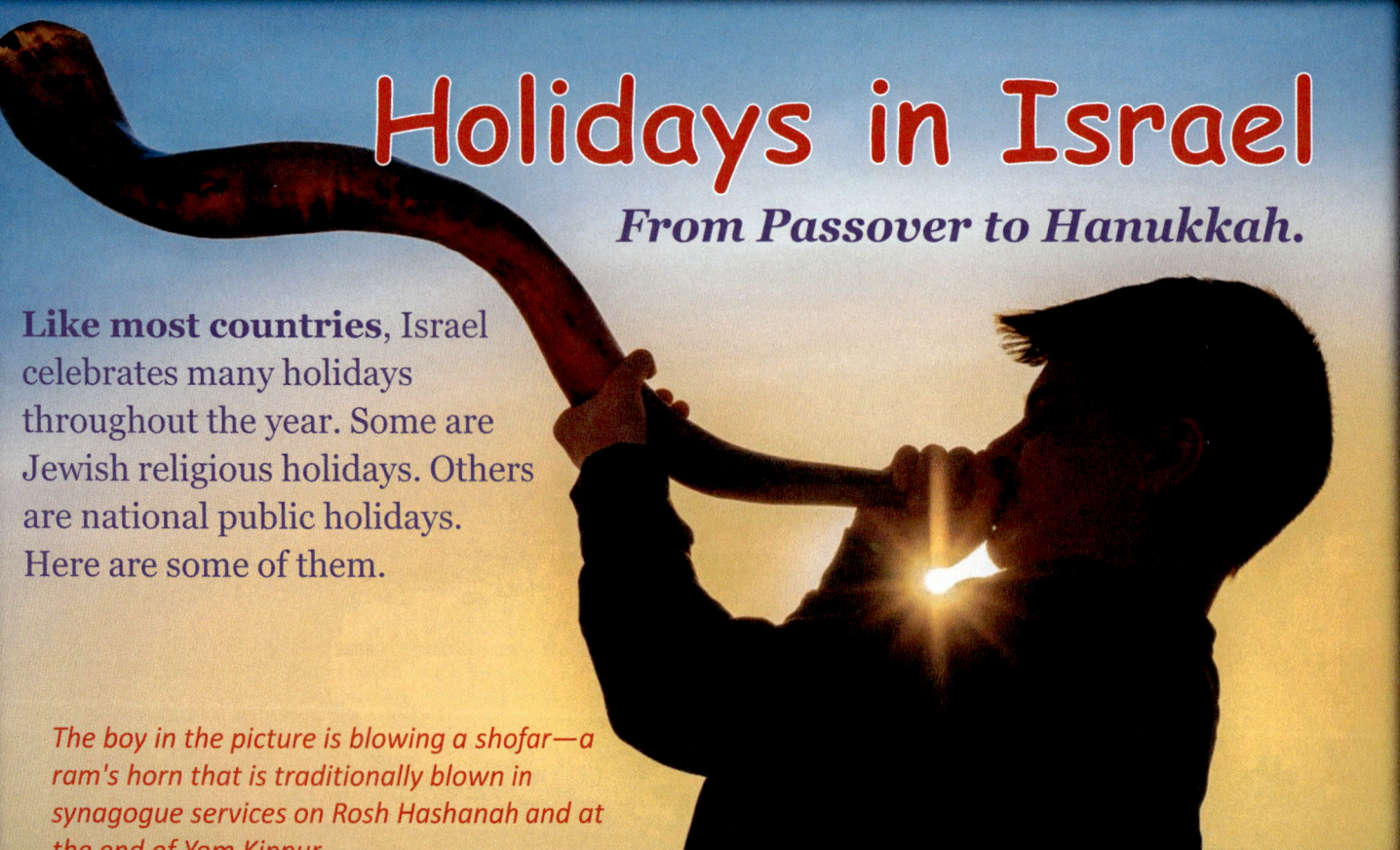

Like most countries, Israel celebrates many holidays throughout the year. Some are Jewish religious holidays. Others are national public holidays. Here are some of them.

The boy in the picture is blowing a shofar—a ram's horn that is traditionally blown in synagogue services on Rosh Hashanah and at the end of Yom Kippur.

Passover (Pesach, *usually March/April)* is a seven-day Jewish holiday that remembers the exodus of the Israelites from slavery in Egypt.

Independence Day (Yom HaAtzmaut, *usually April*) an official national holiday. It commemorates the declaration of independence of Israel in 1948.

Memorial Day (Yom Hazikaron, *usually April*) is a day to honor and remember those who have fallen while on active duty for their country, as well as civilian victims of terrorism.

Rosh Hashanah (Jewish new year, *usually September*) begins a 10-day period known as the High Holy Days (or "10 days of repentance"). Jews across the world ask for forgiveness for their sins. It ends on Yom Kippur.

Yom Kippur (Yom Ha-Kippuri, *September/October*) is the most solemn of Jewish religious holidays. It is known as the Day of Atonement. On Yom Kippur Jews confess their sins to God and pray for His forgiveness.

Hanukkah (*usually December*) is one of the most beautiful Jewish holidays. It celebrates a military victory over foreign rulers more than 2,000 years ago. The holiday lasts for 8 days, and every day a new candle is lit on a Menorah (a candleholder).

The Hebrew Calendar

The Hebrew (or Jewish) calendar is different from the calendar used in the United States and other western countries. That calendar is based on the earth going around the sun.

The Jewish calendar, however, is based on the moon going around the earth. As a result, the holidays begin on a slightly different date each year.

The diagram below shows the months of the Hebrew calendar and approximately when they fall in relation to the months of the Western calendar.

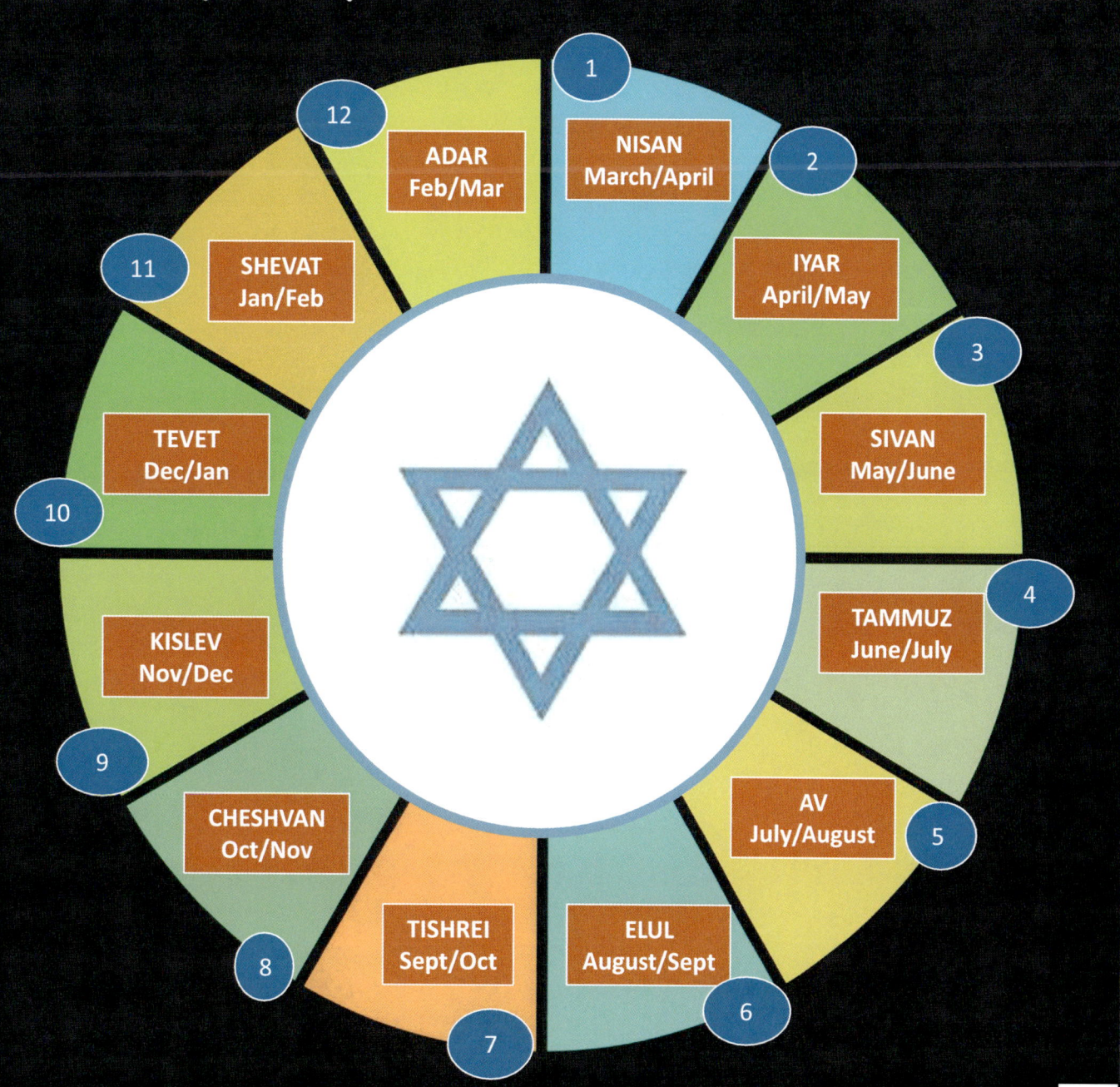

Why do Jews rock back and forth when they pray?

This is a very old custom. It's called shuckling in Yiddish and means to rock, shake, or swing. There are many reasons why some Jews shuckle when praying. Many Jews believe it helps them concentrate or focus on praying and learning. But not all Jews shuckle when they pray.

I heard kids didn't have to go to school in Israel, if they didn't want.

No, that's not true. School in Israel is pretty much like the United States and other Western countries. It consists of primary education (grades 1–6); middle school (grades 7–9); and high school (grades 10–12).

What is the most popular sport in Israel?

Football (what you in the West call soccer) is the official game of Israel and the most popular. But basketball is the second most popular sport in Israel. There is also another unofficial national sport. It's called matkot. It's a traditional beach game of tennis without a net.

Chapter 3

Landmarks and Attractions

Every country has its famous and popular landmarks and attractions.

Some landmarks are made by humans, like the Eiffel Tower in Paris or the Statue of Liberty in the United States. Other landmarks are natural wonders, created over thousands or millions of years. The Grand Canyon in the United States is an example.

Israel also has many famous landmarks and attractions, including many sacred attractions, such as the Western Wall.

People from all over the world come to see the Western Wall and other sacred and unique landmarks and attractions in Israel. Here are some of them.

The Western Wall is about 160 feet (50 meters) long and 60 feet (20 meters) high.

The Biblical Zoo

Its official name is The Tisch Family Zoological Gardens in Jerusalem. But most people simply call it the "Biblical Zoo." That's because the zoo is home to the world's largest collection of animals mentioned in the Bible. It's also home to many endangered species from around the world.

The zoo is spread out over 62 acres in a lovely valley with green hills. It includes a small lake with beautiful waterfalls. The enclosures of the biblical animals feature appropriate Biblical quotes.

Kids can ride a train around the grounds and enjoy an animal-themed play area and petting zoo.

A black-handed spider monkey swings on a rope over the artificial lake at the Jerusalem Biblical Zoo.

Photo Credit: Yoninah

The Dead Sea

The lowest body of water on Earth.

Do you like to float in water?

There's no easier place to do that than in the Dead Sea.

This amazing body of water is almost nine times as salty as the ocean. That makes the water very dense (or thick). The density is what makes it possible for people to float with ease.

The Dead Sea lies between Jordan on the east and Israel and the West Bank on the west. It is 31 mi (50 km) long and 9.3 mi (15 km) wide at its widest point.

The Dead Sea is "dead" because it is impossible for most life to exist in it. You won't find any fish or aquatic plants in the Dead Sea.

But here's the curious thing. The Dead Sea is actually a salt lake, not a sea at all. So why isn't it call the Dead Lake? Good question.

26

Why Is the Dead Sea So Salty?

The land surrounding the Dead Sea is a desert. The hot summer temperatures cause the lake's water to evaporate at a high rate. When the water evaporates it leaves behind salt. Over many years, a high concentration of salt has built up in the Dead Sea.

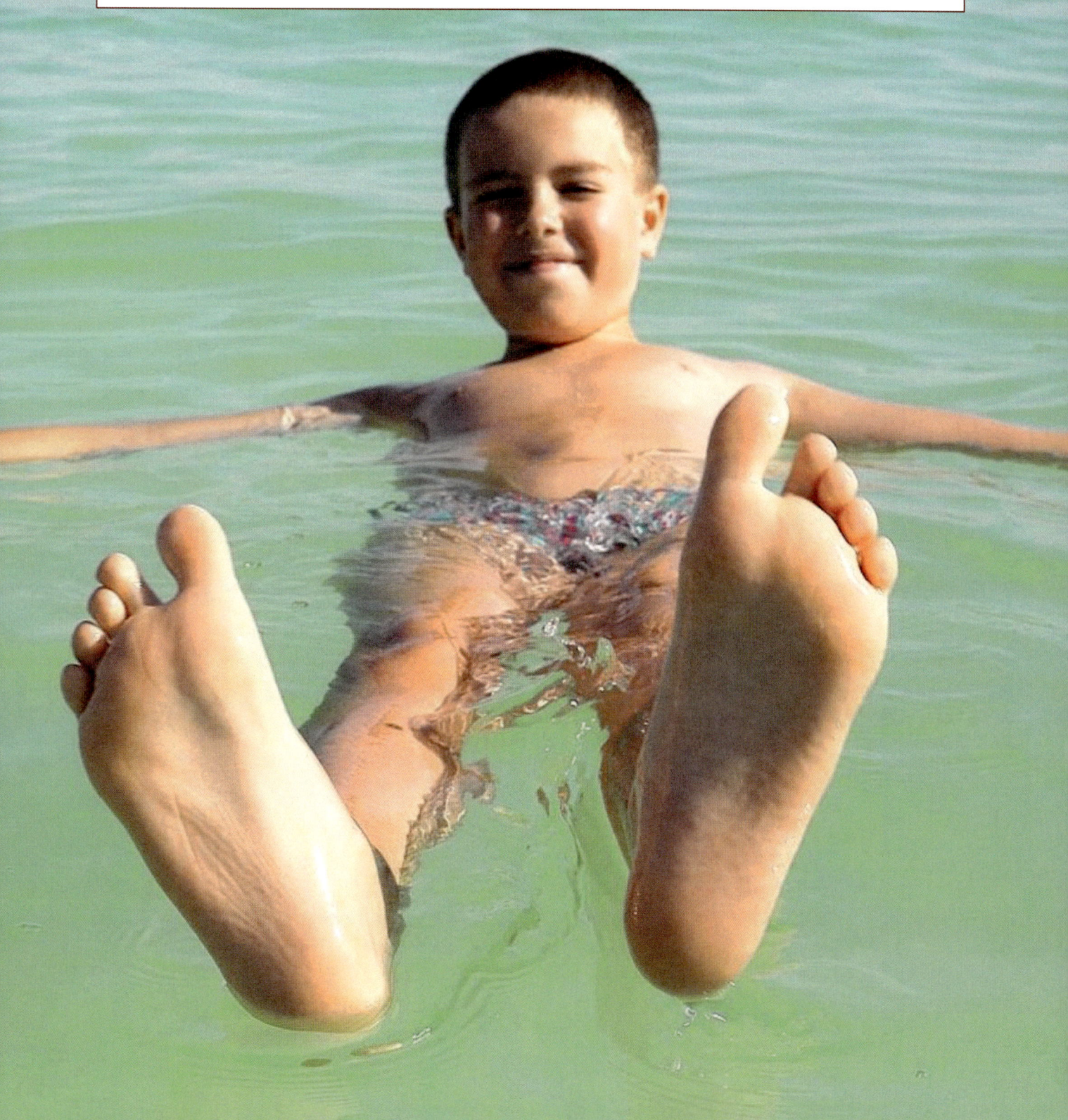

Rosh HaNikra

A spectacular natural phenomenon formed by the sea.

If you like exploring caves, you'll love Rosh HaNikra — an awesome network of grottoes and caves along the Mediterranean coastline between Israel and Lebanon.

Over thousands of years, the sea pounded against the white rocky cliffs, carving out natural grottos and caves.

Today, you can explore the stunning cavities, tunnels, and chambers in the cliffs.

But that's only half the fun. To get to the tunnels and caves you take a colorful cable car. The incline (or slope) is said to be the steepest in the world.

Did You Know?
A grotto is a small natural or artificial cave near water that is often flooded at high tide.

Photo: Chmee2

Masada

An ancient fort, one of Israel's most popular attractions.

Between 37 and 31 BCE, Herod the Great —king of Judea — built a large fortress on top of an isolated rock plateau or mesa, overlooking the Dead Sea.

Herod built the fort as a refuge for him and his family in the event of a revolt. He erected there two palaces, fortifications (military buildings), and other structures.

Today, Masada is one of Israel's most popular tourist attractions. Visitors can walk to the top via the "Snake Path." Or they can take a cable-car to the top. Or go up one way, and down the other. Your choice.

Mini Israel

"See It All — Small."

It may look like the real thing (see below). But, in fact, it's a miniature model — a replica — of the Western Wall in Israel. It is one of more than three hundred historical, cultural and religious sites in a delightful park called, appropriately, "Mini Israel."

These miniature landmarks are located in an eight-acre park between Tel Aviv and Jerusalem. The park is loosely shaped like a star of David with each of the six triangles representing an area or city of Israel.

Some of the miniature landmarks are actually taller than a young child. The famous historical and biblical landmarks are "populated" with thousands of "residents," each no more than about 2.76 inches (7 cm) tall. There are also models of El Al and Swiss Air jets that taxi about on the miniature runway and make some noise, but never take off.

Mini Israel is a great introduction to some of the most famous landmarks, buildings, and structures in Israel. It's a fun way to learn about Israel for kids and their parents, too.

A replica of the Western Wall in miniature at "Mini Israel."

A miniature model of the Western Wall and Dome of the Rock at Mini Israel.

Ramat Gan Safari

"Africa in the heart of Israel."

Imagine an African safari in Israel.

Actually, you don't have to imagine it. You can have an (almost) authentic African safari experience at the Ramat Gan Safari.

The Ramat Gan Safari is located on 250 acres of nature in the city of Ramat Gan, just four miles (six kilometers) from Tel Aviv.

The zoo is officially known as the Zoological Center Tel Aviv-Ramat Gan. It is said to have the largest collection of wildlife in human care in the Middle East. That includes white rhinos, hippos, lions, African and Asian elephants, gorillas, orangutans, and even these two little guys (*see below*). No wonder why the zoo is nicknamed "Africa in the heart of Israel."

Just like in their natural habitats, the animals roam freely in large herds. Like on any other safari, you can watch these animals eating, playing, and sleeping—all in their natural habitat.

Two meerkats at the Ramat Gan's Safari

Eilat's Coral World Underwater Observatory

The biggest public aquarium in Israel.

Just for fun, how would like to . . .

√ Come eye-to-eye with sharks, sting-rays, and other predators of the Red Sea?

√ Enjoy watching the behavior of sea turtles both in water and on land, as they swim, feed and go about their daily lives?

√ Discover the many secrets of the fascinating humpback whales?

√ Check out more than 800 species of rare and beautiful fish, coral, and spectacular marine creatures?

√ Go underwater and see an authentic reef in the Red Sea without getting wet?

You can do all those things and more at Eilat's Coral World Underwater Observatory. It's the only active underwater observatory in the world, located in Eilat, Israel. It is the biggest public aquarium in Israel, and it hosts over 800 species.

An underwater tunnel at Eilat's Coral World Underwater Observatory provides an up-close and personal look at twenty shark species, rays, and corals.
Photo: Dr. Avishai Teicher Pikiwiki Israel

Chapter 4
The Wildlife of Israel

Israel is a small country. Yet, it has many different landscapes, from snow-covered mountains to dry, hot deserts to lush woodlands.

All of these landscapes provide a home to a wide variety of wildlife. In fact, there are 116 species of mammals native to Israel, 511 kinds of birds, 97 types of reptiles, and seven types of amphibians.

Today, the largest land animals are mountain gazelles, wild boar, foxes, jungle cats, and Nubian ibex. There are also leopards, hyenas, jackals and wolves. But people rarely see them.

Here are just a few of the many different animals that make Israel their home.

Fun Fact

The continent of Europe is about 300 times larger in size than Israel. Yet, Israel has 116 different species of land animals, while all of Europe has only slightly more — 140 different species.

Israeli Gazelle

The national animal of Israel.

ISRAELI GAZELLE
At a Glance

AKA: Mountain gazelle

Length: Male: 40-45 in (101-115 cm); female: 38.5-40 (98-101 cm).

Height: 2–3.5 ft (60-110 cm) high at the shoulder.

Weight: Male: (17-29.5 kgs); female: (16-25 kgs).

Lifespan: 8-15 years.

Diet: Herbivorous: herbs and shrubs in the summer and green grasses in the winter.

Conservation Status: Endangered.

Gazelles are smaller relatives of the antelope.

There are many different species of antelope. Until recently, gazelles living in Israel and Palestine were considered part of the mountain gazelle species.

But then scientists made an interesting discovery. The gazelles living in Israel and the Palestinian territories are a separate species. They just happen to look a lot like all the other gazelles.

Today, one of the best places to see this mountain gazelle is in Gazelle Valley. It's described as Israel's first urban nature reserve. Several endangered species other than gazelles live in the Gazelle Valley.

Arabian Oryx

From extinct to vulnerable in 40 years.

At the beginning of the 1970s, the Arabian oryx was considered extinct. Scientists thought it no longer existed in the wild. Yet, by 2012, this medium-sized antelope was considered only vulnerable. That means it went from extinct in the wild to critically endangered to endangered to vulnerable – all in a period of about forty years.

Scientists were amazed. It is the only animal to go from extinct in the wild to vulnerable. Scientists were also very happy. If the Arabian oryx could go from extinct to vulnerable, maybe other animals could do the same.

ARABIAN ORYX
At a Glance

AKA: The white oryx

What It Is: A species of antelope.

Height: 39 in (1 m) at the shoulder.

Weight: 150 lb (70 kg).

Horns: 20 to 30 in (50 to 75 cm) long.

Diet: Mainly grasses, but also buds, herbs, fruit, tubers and roots.

Lifespan: Up to 20 years (in captivity).

Predator: Wolves, humans.

Conservation Status: Vulnerable.

The Deathstalker

One of the most dangerous scorpions in the world.

A sting from this scorpion may not actually kill someone (despite its name), but it sure would be painful. Its scientific name in English means "five-striped, smooth-tail." Take a look at the picture. Is that a good name for it?

Some doctors believe a component of the Deathstalker's venom may help in treating brain tumors and possibly diabetes.

Deathstalker, Negev desert, Israel

THE DEATHSTALKER
At a Glance

AKA: The Yellow Scorpion

Length: 1.2–3.0 in (30–77 millimeters) long.

Weight: 2.5 grams (28 grams equal an ounce, so these critters are pretty lightweight).

Diet: Insects, some types of spiders, earthworms, centipedes and also other scorpions.

Fun Fact

A scorpion has two eyes on the top of its head and often two to five pairs of eyes on the front corners of its head.

The Nile Soft-Shelled Turtle

The largest freshwater turtle in the world.

If you'd like to see giant soft-shelled turtles in Israel, there's really only one place to go — the Nahal Alexander River. The river is only about 28 miles (45 km) long. But it's the best place in Israel to find soft shell turtles which are almost as long as the average ten-year-old is tall.

NILE SOFT-SHELLED TURTLE
At a Glance

AKA: The African Soft-Shelled Turtle

Length: 33 to 37 inches (85 to 95 cm).

Weight: Up to 32 lb (50 kilograms)

Diet: Carnivorous: amphibians, crustaceans, fish, insects, small mammals, mollusks, and worms.

Lifespan: 25 to 45 years.

Conservation Status: Critically endangered.

Fun Fact

The elongated head of the soft-shelled turtle ends in small, snorkel like nostrils.

Arabian Leopard

The only type of leopard to live in Israel.

Of all the different kinds (or species) of leopards in the world, the Arabian leopard is the smallest. Sadly, it is on the verge of extinction. Researchers estimate there are fewer than 200 Arabian Leopards anywhere in the wild. A 2006 study found evidence of just eight Arabian leopards in a small area of Israel. There have been no sightings since then.

Is the Arabian leopard now extinct? Hopefully not. Maybe, like the Arabian Oryx, scientists will one day discover the Arabian Leopard has survived in Israel.

ARABIAN LEOPARD
At a Glance

Length: Male: 72–80 in (182–203 cm), including 30–33 in (77–85 cm) long tail; female: 63–76 in (160–192 cm) long, 26–31 in (67–79 cm) long tail.

Weight: Male: 66 lb (30 kg); female: 44 lb (20 kg).

Height: 17.7-31.4 in (45-80 cm) at the shoulder.

Diet: Carnivorous: Nubian ibex, porcupine, foxes, snakes, lizards, and rodents.

Lifespan: Up to twenty years.

Conservation Status: Critically endangered; possibly extinct in Israel.

Hoopoe

The national bird of Israel.

In 2008, Israel wanted to choose a national bird. So, the country conducted a survey.

"What bird should represent Israel?" the survey asked.

More than 150,000 people responded. And the winner? The Hoopoe, a magnificent orange bird with zebra-striped wings, an amazing "crown" of feathers, and a long, thin bill.

So, who was the runner-up? Find out on page 43.

THE HOOPOE
At a Glance

Length: 10 in. – 12.6 in. (25 cm – 32 cm).

Wingspan: 17-19 in (44 cm – 48 cm).

Weight: 1.6 oz – 3.1 oz (46g – 89g)

Diet: Insects, frogs, and reptiles.

Lifespan: Around 10 years in the wild.

Conservation Status: Least concern (for now).

Fun Fact

The hoopoe gets its name from its distinctive call, which sounds like "hooo-pooo."

Marbled Polecat

Poor eyesight but a good sense of smell.

Look at that face. It's about as cute as any small animal around, right?

In 1996, IUCN Red List considered the marbled polecat a species of least concern. But guess what?

Twelve years later, in 2008, the marbled polecat was classified as a vulnerable.

Scientists believe the population of the polecat declined (went down) for two reasons: First, because of construction, the polecat lost much of its habitat. Secondly, the widespread use of rodenticides (chemicals used to kill small rodents) killed much of the food source (or prey) for the polecat.

MARBLED POLECAT
At a Glance

Length: 11 – 14 in (29–35 cm).

Weight: Males from 11.3 to 25.2 oz (320 to 715 g); females from 10.4 to 21.2 oz (295 to 600 g).,

Diet: Carnivorous. They eat ground squirrels, hamsters, rats, house mice, and other rodents, small hares, birds, lizards and crickets).

Lifespan: Up to 14 years in captivity, five years or so in the wild.

Conservation Status: Vulnerable.

Fun Fact

Like a skunk, the marbled polecat emits (sends out or gives off) a strong smell from under its tail when threatened.

THE IUCN RED LIST

The Conservation Status of Animals.

The IUCN Red List is a special list of thousands of animal species. The list tells how likely it is that each animal on the list might become extinct in the future. This is called the animal's *conservation status*.

Animals are classified in seven main groups. The groups are listed below, along with an example of an animal in each group.

Extinct (EX): No longer exists.

Example: Dodo bird.

Extinct in the Wild (EW): Only exists in captivity (e.g., zoos)

Example: Hawaiian crow, Scimitar oryx.

Critically Endangered (CR): At very high risk of extinction

Example: Western lowland gorilla, hirola (world's rarest antelope).

Endangered (EN): High risk of extinction in the wild.

Example: Siberian tiger, brown spider monkey.

Vulnerable (VU): High risk of endangerment in the wild.

Example: blue crane, yak.

Near Threatened (NT): Likely to become endangered in the near future.

Example: European otter, maned wolf.

Least Concern (LC): Lowest risk.

Example: More than 30,000 animal species in this group.

ANSWER FROM PAGE 40: RUNNER-UP:

What bird came in second in a contest to vote for a national bird of Israel?

Answer: The White-Spectacled Bulbul

Photo: : Baresi franco

Thank you for reading about my amazing country. Come visit us sometime!

For other fun-to-read books about countries and cultures around the world, visit www.curiouskidspress.com

Explore the World

Find these books on Amazon.com
Preview them (and more) at curiouskidspress.com

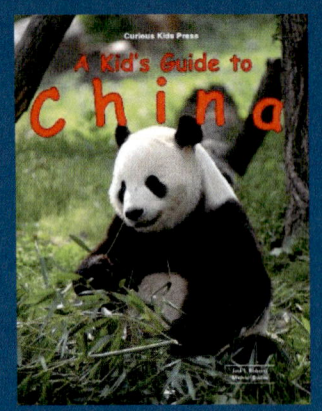

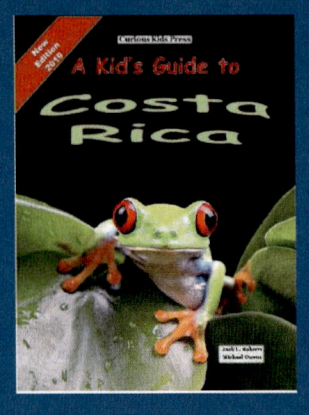

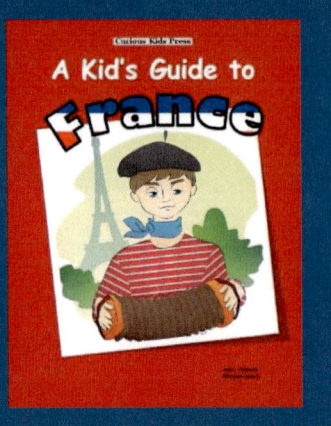

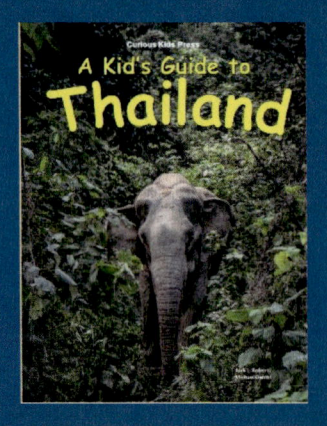

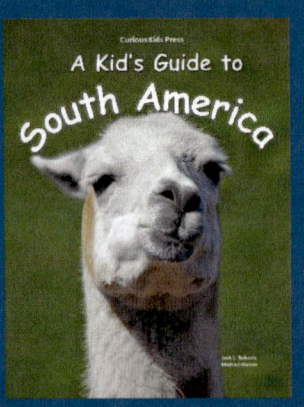

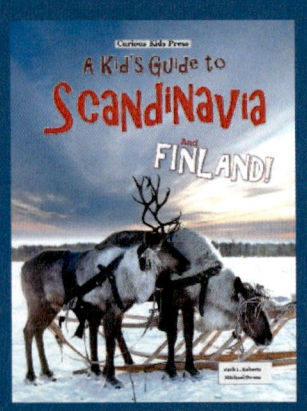

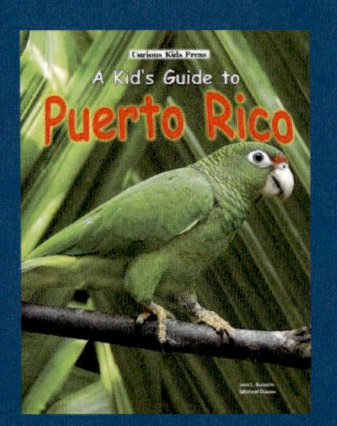

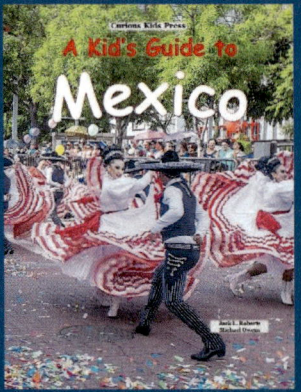

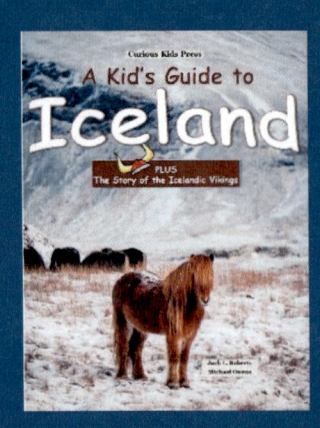

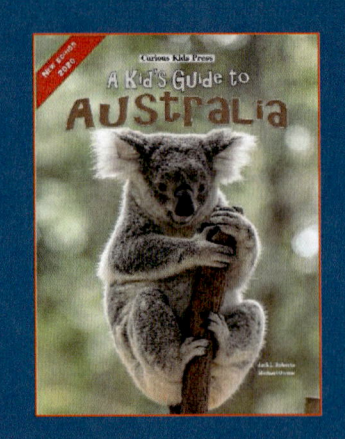

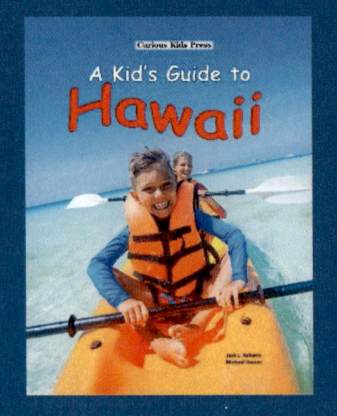

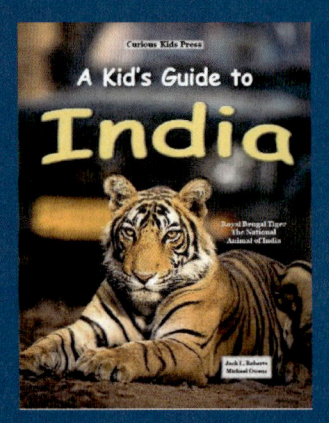

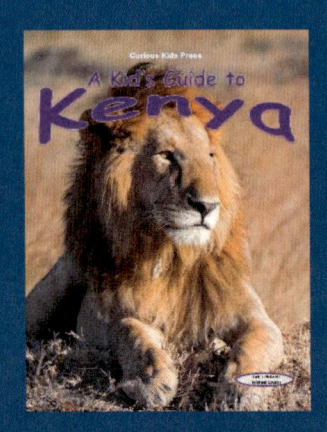

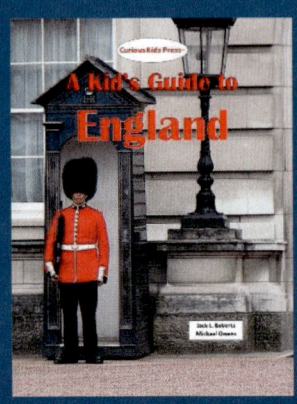

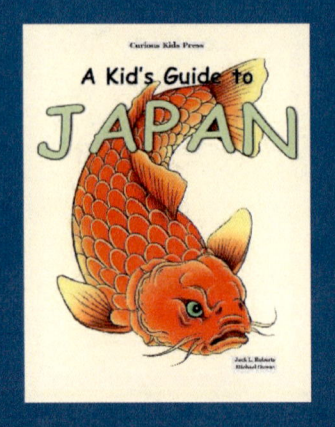

A Kid's Guide to China
A Kid's Guide to Costa Rica
A Kid's Guide to France
A Kid's Guide to Thailand

A Kid's Guide to South America
A Kid's Guide to Scandinavia and Finland
A Kid's Guide to Puerto Rico
A Kid's Guide to Mexico

A Kid's Guide to Iceland — Plus The Story of the Icelandic Vikings
A Kid's Guide to Australia
A Kid's Guide to Hawaii
A Kid's Guide to India

A Kid's Guide to Kenya
A Kid's Guide to England
A Kid's Guide to Japan
A Kid's Guide to Alaska

Curious Kids Press
www.curiouskidspress.com

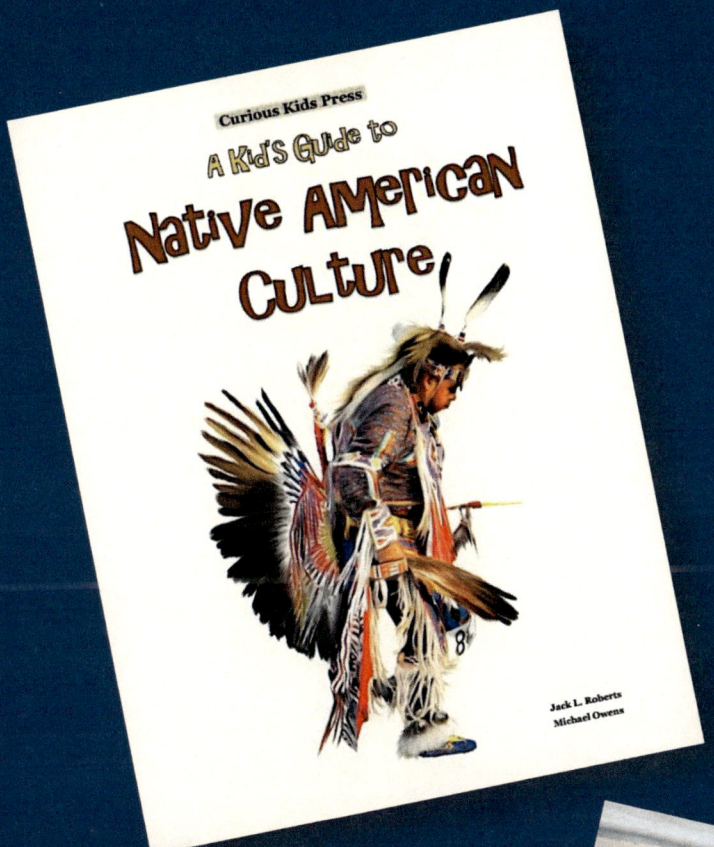

Two important new books for all young readers and their families.

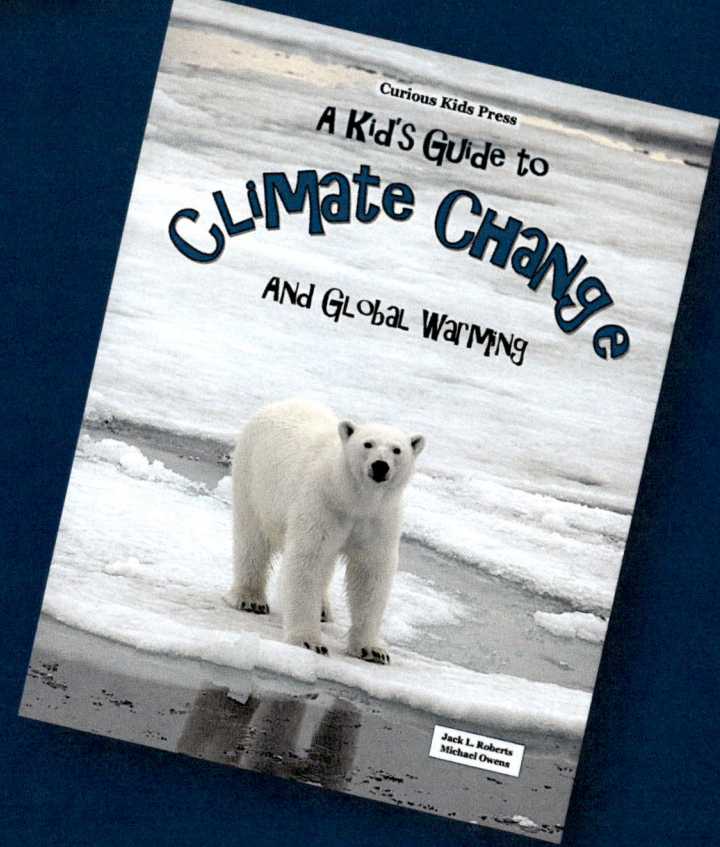

Available on amazon.com

A Kid's Guide to
Israel
For Parents and Teachers

About This Book

A Kid's Guide to . . . is an engaging, easy-to-read book series that provides an exciting adventure into fascinating countries and cultures around the world for young readers. Each book focuses on one country, continent, or U.S. territory or state, and includes colorful photographs, informational charts and graphs, and quirky and bizarre "Did You Know" facts, all designed to bring the country and its people to life. Designed primarily for recreational, high-interest reading, the informational text series is also a great resource for students to use to research geography topics or writing assignments.

About the Reading Level

A Kid's Guide to . . . is an informational text series designed for kids in grades 4 to 6, ages 9 to 12. For some young readers, the series will provide new reading challenges based on the vocabulary and sentence structure. For other readers, the series will review and reinforce reading skills already achieved. While for still other readers, the book will match their current skill level, regardless of age or grade level.

About the Authors

Jack L. Roberts began his career in educational publishing at Children's Television Workshop (now Sesame Workshop), where he was Senior Editor of The Sesame Street/Electric Company Reading Kits. Later, at Scholastic Inc., he was the founding editor of a high-interest/low-reading level magazine for middle school students. He also founded two technology magazines for teachers and administrators.

Roberts is the author of more than two dozen biographies and other nonfiction titles for young readers, published by Scholastic Inc., the Lerner Publishing Group, Teacher Created Materials, Benchmark Education, and others.. More recently, he was the co-founder of WordTeasers, an educational series of card decks designed to help kids of all ages improve their vocabulary through "conversation, not memorization."

Michael Owens is a noted jazz dance teacher, award-winning wildlife photographer, graphic arts designer, and devoted animal lover.

In 2017, Roberts and Owens launched Curious Kids Press (CKP), an educational publishing company focused on publishing high-interest, nonfiction books for young readers, primarily books about countries and cultures around the world. Currently, CKP has published two series of country books: "A Kid's Guide to..." (for ages 9-12 and "Let's Visit . . ." (for ages 6-8) — both designed to help young readers explore the wonderful world of diversity in everything from food and holidays to geography and traditions.

To Our Valued Customers

Curious Kids Press is passionate about creating fun-to-read books about countries and cultures around the world for young readers, and we work hard every day to create quality products.

All of our books are Print on Demand books. As a result, on rare occasions, you may find minor printing errors. If you feel you have not received a quality printed product, please send us a description and photo of the printing error along with your name and address and we will have a new copy sent to you free of charge. Contact us at: info@curiouskidspress.com

Made in the USA
Las Vegas, NV
05 September 2023